VIRAL LAWYER

How to Make Videos so Good
People Feel Stupid Scrolling Past

Mike Kruzich

Table of Contents

Introduction

Short Form Videos - A Revolutionary Approach to Personal Injury Law Practice

Hello, and welcome to the vanguard of social media and legal practice intermingling. If you're a personal injury lawyer with a desire to evolve with the digital age and reach a broader, more engaged audience, then you're in the right place. As a social media expert with a following of 5 million and over 2 billion total views, I've witnessed firsthand the transformative power of short form video content.

In this cutting-edge guide, we're going to delve deep into the world of short form videos and its potential to revolutionize your law practice. This isn't about fleeting trends or gimmicks; this is about harnessing the genuine power of storytelling and human connection to elevate your practice and better serve your clients.

Over the years, I've watched as personal injury lawyers grappled with the challenge of translating complex legal narratives into digestible content for the average social media user. The solution lies not in oversimplification, but in the art of micro-storytelling - distilling the essence of your client's experience into a compelling, bite-sized narrative that speaks to the heart of your audience.

Short form video content, like TikTok, Instagram Reels, and other emerging platforms, offers a unique opportunity to do just that. However, the secret to success isn't just in the medium; it's in the

Email me directly at mike@mikekruzich.com if you would like me to personally assess your Lawfirm's social media presence.

1

message, the delivery, and the understanding of the platform's unique mechanics.

This book is designed to guide you through the process of creating impactful short form video content. It will arm you with the strategies and tools you need to stand out in a crowded digital landscape, earn the trust and admiration of your audience, and position yourself as a leading voice in the personal injury law space.

From mastering the art of the hook to understanding social algorithms, and from leveraging testimonials to future-proofing your video content strategy, each chapter of this book is carefully crafted to empower you to navigate the ever-changing social media landscape confidently.

Whether you're just getting started on social media or you're looking to breathe new life into your existing online presence, this book is your roadmap to success. It's not just about gaining followers; it's about building meaningful connections, asserting your expertise, and amplifying your clients' voices.

So, let's embark on this journey together, shattering traditional notions of legal practice, and embracing the transformative power of short form videos. Get ready to make a lasting impact, one micro-story at a time.

Bonus: email me directly at mike@mikekruzich.com if you would like me to personally assess your Lawfirm's social media presence or if you have any questions.

Email me directly at mike@mikekruzich.com if you
would like me to personally assess your Lawfirm's social media presence

3

Chapter 1

The Power of the Micro-Story: Translating Personal Injury Cases into Short Form Videos

Welcome to the digital age. A time when the human attention span has shrunk to less than that of a goldfish, and where an individual's story can be told, shared, and go viral in less time than it takes to drink a cup of coffee. The currency of this era? Short form video content.

Short form videos have quickly become the driving force behind social media engagement. They offer a unique opportunity for personal injury lawyers to craft captivating narratives about their clients' experiences, demonstrating their prowess in fighting for justice, all while reaching a broader audience than ever before.

Translating personal injury cases into compelling short form videos may seem like an uphill task, given the complexity and nuance that these cases often carry. However, with the right approach, you can distill these intricate narratives into bite-sized content that not only resonates with your audience but also leaves a lasting impact.

The power of a micro-story lies in its ability to connect with viewers on a human level. Each case you handle is more than just a legal proceeding; it's a person's life significantly impacted by an unfortunate event. It's a story of perseverance, resilience, and the pursuit of justice.

Let's start with a straightforward concept: the 3C's of a compelling micro-story - Context, Conflict, and Conclusion.

Context sets the stage, introducing the characters and their circumstances. In a personal injury case, this could be a brief background of your client and the event leading to the injury.

Conflict is the heart of the story. It involves the struggles, obstacles, or challenges faced by your client. This is where you portray the magnitude of the issue and how it disrupted your client's life.

The Conclusion wraps up the story. It could be a successful settlement, a court verdict in your client's favor, or even an ongoing case seeking justice. It's also the moment to highlight your role in their journey towards justice.

Remember, your goal is to evoke emotions and build a connection. You're not lecturing about the law; you're narrating a human story. Let's consider an example:

Context: "Meet John, a construction worker with three young kids, who was severely injured due to a scaffolding collapse at his worksite."

Conflict: "John faced mounting medical bills, loss of income, and a daunting legal battle against a corporation that claimed no responsibility."

Email me directly at mike@mikekruzich.com if you would like me to personally assess your Lawfirm's social media presence

5

Conclusion: "With our relentless pursuit for justice, we secured a fair settlement for John, helping him cover his medical bills, provide for his family, and start a new chapter in his life."

The above narrative is simple yet powerful. It doesn't delve into intricate legal details but highlights the human aspect of the case, which is what truly resonates with viewers.

As you embark on your short form video journey, remember that you're not just a lawyer in these videos; you're a storyteller, an advocate, and a beacon of hope for individuals who've experienced personal hardships due to others' negligence. Your videos are your stage, your cases are your scripts, and your clients are your protagonists.

In the coming chapters, we will delve deeper into the practical aspects of creating short form videos, right from capturing attention in the first few seconds to building your brand identity and understanding social media algorithms.

The revolution of short form videos in personal injury law practice is here, and you're at the forefront of it. Embrace it, master it, and let the power of the micro-story elevate your practice to new heights.

Chapter 2

The Art of the Hook: Capturing Attention in the First 5 Seconds

In the fast-paced realm of social media, the first few seconds of your video can make or break its success. It's a landscape where users are constantly scrolling, deciding in mere moments whether to engage with a piece of content or move on to the next. This is where the art of the hook comes into play.

A 'hook' is an opening that instantly grabs the viewer's attention, kindling their curiosity, and compelling them to watch the rest of your video. It's your first impression, your elevator pitch, and your golden ticket to engagement.

In the context of personal injury law, crafting a compelling hook can be particularly challenging. The subject matter is often complex and sensitive, and your audience is diverse. But don't let this daunt you. With the right strategy, you can create powerful hooks that resonate with your audience, showcase your expertise, and set the stage for your micro-story.

Here are some strategies for crafting a compelling hook for your short form videos:

1. Start with a Question: Questions provoke thought and engagement. They urge the viewer to pause and consider an

answer. For instance, "Have you ever wondered what to do immediately after a car accident?"

2. Showcase a Strong Statement: Bold declarations can instantly grab attention and express the essence of your video. For example, "Injustice met its match when we took on this corporate giant."

3. Use Visual Intrigue: A striking visual element or an action that defies expectation can pull viewers in. This could be a re-enactment, a relevant animation, or even a dramatic representation of a case.

4. Tease the Outcome: Hinting at a significant event or result can pique curiosity. "Watch how we turned a denied claim into a six-figure settlement."

5. Incorporate Empathy: Connect on an emotional level. Show that you understand the struggles your clients go through. "When an injury turned John's life upside down, we were there to help him get back on his feet."

Each video you create has a unique narrative, and your hook should reflect that. It should be a sneak peek into the story that you're about to unfold, a promise of value, or a hint of the emotion that your video will evoke.

Remember, the goal of the hook isn't just to stop the scroll; it's to captivate the viewer and make them eager to watch the rest of your video. It's your first step in connecting with your audience, building trust, and asserting your position as an advocate for justice.

In the next chapter, we will explore the concept of 'microcontent,' the creation of meaningful, value-packed content within the constraints of short form video. As you continue to evolve your video strategy, remember that every second counts, and every moment is an opportunity to resonate with your audience.

Master the art of the hook, and you've won half the battle in the arena of short form video content.

Email me directly at mike@mikekruzich.com if you
would like me to personally assess your Lawfirm's social media presence

9

Chapter 3

Hero, Hub, Help: A Triad Strategy for Compelling Content Creation

The digital landscape, teeming with content, is competitive and relentless. It requires a well-crafted strategy, enabling you to stand out and appeal to your audience. The 'Hero, Hub, Help' content model is a proven approach that leverages a mix of content types to create a comprehensive and effective digital strategy.

Understanding the Hero, Hub, Help Model

The essence of this model lies in its triadic structure: Hero, Hub, and Help, each representing a different content type designed to engage your audience at varying levels of their journey.

1. Hero Content: This is the blockbuster of your content strategy. These are the high-impact, high-production-value pieces often centered around an event or a campaign. They're aimed at a broad audience and designed to create maximum visibility and virality.

2. Hub Content: This is the episodic, regularly scheduled content that keeps your followers coming back. Hub content nurtures your existing audience, keeping them engaged, educated, and entertained.

3. Help Content: This is the answer to your audience's questions. Help content builds your credibility as an expert in your field and caters to those actively seeking information or solutions in your domain.

A Personal Injury Lawyer's Take on Hero, Hub, Help

Let's explore how you, as a personal injury lawyer, can implement this strategy with short-form videos, using a true story.

Meet Jane Smith, a personal injury lawyer who was just starting her journey on social media. She knew she needed to create compelling content, but she was struggling to break through the noise and reach her desired audience. Then she stumbled upon the 'Hero, Hub, Help' model, and her social media strategy transformed.

1. Hero: Jane decided to kickstart her TikTok presence by creating a high-impact short video around the 'Day in the Life of a Personal Injury Lawyer.' She went all out, from her morning routine, through the rigors of court cases, to her after-work activities. The video garnered over 1 million views, giving Jane's TikTok account a great head start.

2. Hub: With her followers now numbering in the thousands, Jane embarked on creating a series of 'Law Explained in 60 seconds' videos. This served as her Hub content, drawing her followers back with consistent, valuable insights about the legal world.

Email me directly at mike@mikekruzich.com if you would like me to personally assess your Lawfirm's social media presence

11

3. Help: As her following grew, Jane noticed a recurring theme in the questions and comments: people needed advice on what to do immediately after an accident. To address this, Jane created 'post-accident guide' videos, offering clear, actionable advice - her Help content.

Jane's story illuminates the power of the 'Hero, Hub, Help' content strategy, particularly in the domain of short-form video content. Remember, your strategy need not be set in stone; adapt it based on your audience's response. Keep experimenting with different formats and content themes within each category to see what resonates most with your audience.

In the end, the 'Hero, Hub, Help' strategy is about balance. Just as a stool needs all three legs to stand, your content strategy should utilize all three forms of content. So start brainstorming your Hero, Hub, and Help content, and prepare to see your social media presence soar.

Chapter 4

Mastery of Microcontent: Inspiring Engagement in the Legal Sphere

In the realm of social media, 'microcontent' has emerged as a powerful vehicle for engagement. This term refers to short, easily digestible pieces of content that deliver value in a compact package. The challenge – and indeed, the art – lies in distilling complex ideas into a format that not only fits within the time constraints of short form videos but also resonates with your audience.

As a personal injury lawyer, your subject matter can be complex and multifaceted. The task of simplifying these concepts without losing their essence can seem daunting. However, with a deep understanding of your audience and a strategic approach to content creation, you can master the art of microcontent.

Here are key strategies to inspire engagement in the legal sphere through microcontent:

1. Focus on One Core Idea: Each video should revolve around a single, clear concept. Whether it's explaining a legal term, showcasing a case study, or providing advice, make sure your video is focused and concise.

2. Prioritize Value: Every piece of content should provide something of value to your audience. This could be knowledge,

inspiration, a solution to a problem, or even entertainment. The value you provide is the currency that earns you engagement and loyalty.

3. Use Plain Language: Avoid legal jargon and complex language. Your goal is to make your content accessible and understandable to the average person. Remember, simplicity doesn't undermine your expertise; it amplifies your message.

4. Leverage Visuals: Utilize graphics, animations, and other visual elements to enhance understanding. A well-placed visual can often convey a concept more effectively than words alone.

5. Spark Conversation: Encourage your audience to engage with your content. This could be through a question at the end of your video, a call to action to share their experiences, or an invitation to suggest topics for future content.

6. Show, Don't Just Tell: Use storytelling techniques to illustrate your point. Real-life examples, case studies, and client testimonials can make abstract legal concepts more relatable.

7. Keep it Human: Never lose sight of the human element in your videos. Emotion drives engagement. Show empathy, celebrate victories, and remind your audience that behind every case is a person seeking justice.

The mastery of microcontent isn't just about brevity; it's about impact. It's about using each second of your video to make a connection, convey a message, and leave a lasting impression. As a personal injury lawyer, your microcontent isn't just a tool for engagement; it's a platform for education, advocacy, and influence.

In the next chapter, we will delve into the concept of building your brand identity through short form videos. As you continue to hone your microcontent skills, remember that each piece of content is a brick in the monument of your digital identity. Each video is an opportunity to showcase your expertise, reinforce your values, and demonstrate your commitment to your clients. So, use every second wisely and remember, less is often more.

Chapter 5

Your Firm in a Flash: Building Your Brand Identity through Short Form Videos

The digital age has redefined the concept of branding, particularly for the legal profession. It's no longer just about a logo, a catchy tagline, or a polished website. In the dynamic and interactive landscape of social media, brand identity extends to the experiences you provide, the stories you tell, and the values you uphold. In essence, your brand is the personality of your practice and the promise you make to your clients.

Short form videos provide a unique canvas for personal injury lawyers to paint their brand identity. They allow you to show your firm's human side, demonstrate your expertise, and connect with your audience on a personal level. But how do you translate the complexity of your practice and the richness of your client stories into bite-sized videos that accurately represent your brand?

Let's explore the strategies that can help you build a powerful brand identity through short form videos.

1. Define Your Brand Personality:

   Every brand has a personality, a human-like set of traits that define its character. Is your firm empathetic and compassionate, aggressive and relentless, or perhaps innovative and forward-thinking? Your brand personality should reflect in your video

Email me directly at mike@mikekruzich.com if you would like me to personally assess your Lawfirm's social media presence.

16

content, from the tone of your narration to the style of your visuals. This consistency fosters familiarity and trust among your audience.

2. Showcase Your Expertise:

   Short form videos are an excellent platform to demonstrate your knowledge and skills. Explain legal concepts, discuss recent case laws, or share insights on common personal injury questions. When viewers see you as a valuable source of information, they'll associate your brand with expertise and reliability.

3. Tell Client Stories:

   There's no better way to illustrate your brand's values than through the experiences of your clients. With their consent, share their stories, their struggles, and how your firm made a difference in their lives. These narratives humanize your brand and foster emotional connections with your audience.

4. Highlight Your Team:

   Your team is a crucial part of your brand identity. Showcase the people who work tirelessly behind the scenes to fight for your clients. This not only creates a sense of camaraderie but also reinforces your brand as a collective of dedicated professionals.

5. Leverage Testimonials:

Email me directly at mike@mikekruzich.com if you would like me to personally assess your Lawfirm's social media presence

17

Happy clients are the best brand ambassadors. Share short testimonials from clients who've had positive experiences with your firm. These snippets of praise can significantly boost your credibility and reputation.

6. Be Consistent:

Consistency is key in brand building. From the color scheme and logo placement to the tone of voice and message, ensure there's a consistent theme across all your videos. This enhances recognition and strengthens your brand image.

7. Communicate Your 'Why':

Why do you do what you do? What drives you to fight for justice for your clients? This 'why' is the soul of your brand, and it should echo in your video content. Whether it's a belief in fairness, a desire to help others, or a passion for justice, let your 'why' shine through.

8. Engage with Your Audience:

Branding is not a one-way street. Engage with your viewers by responding to comments, addressing their questions, or simply thanking them for their support. This fosters a sense of community and shows your audience that there are real, caring people behind your brand.

Building your brand identity through short form videos is not an overnight process. It requires strategy, consistency, and a genuine understanding of your audience. But the effort is worthwhile. A strong brand can set you apart from the competition, attract your ideal clients, and ultimately, drive the success of your practice.

Remember, your brand is more than a representation of your firm; it's a commitment to your clients. It's the pledge of professionalism, compassion, and relentless advocacy they can expect when they engage with your firm. Short form videos give you the opportunity to bring this commitment to life, to show your audience who you are, what you stand for, and how you champion the cause of justice for your clients.

9. Emphasize Your Unique Selling Proposition (USP):

Your USP is what sets you apart from other personal injury lawyers. It could be your unique approach to case preparation, your track record of successful verdicts, or your specialized expertise in a particular area of personal injury law. Whatever it is, make sure your USP shines through your short form videos.

10. Be Authentic:

Authenticity is the cornerstone of a powerful brand identity. Be true to your firm's values and mission. Avoid imitating trends that don't align with your brand personality. Authenticity resonates with audiences and fosters trust more than any polished facade.

11. Experiment and Evolve:

Digital branding is a dynamic process. Don't be afraid to experiment with different video formats, storytelling techniques, or visual styles. Monitor your audience's response, learn from your successes and failures, and continuously evolve your strategy to better connect with your audience.

In the next chapter, we will explore the power of testimonials in shaping your brand identity and driving client engagement. As we delve deeper into this journey of building your brand through short form videos, remember that your brand is the bridge between your firm and your audience. It's the lens through which they see your practice, the thread that connects them to your stories, and the beacon that guides them to choose you as their advocate in their quest for justice.

So, let every short form video you create be a testament to your brand, a reflection of your commitment, and a beacon of your expertise. In this ever-evolving digital landscape, your brand is not just your identity; it's your legacy.

Chapter 6

Reshaping Legal Landscapes: The Impact of Social Media on Personal Injury Law Practice

As we delve deeper into the realm of social media and short form videos, it's critical to understand the profound impact these platforms are having on the practice of personal injury law. The legal profession, once primarily driven by face-to-face interactions and lengthy documents, is being reshaped by the dynamic, interactive, and visual nature of social media.

From client acquisition and community engagement to case presentation and brand building, social media platforms are revolutionizing the way personal injury lawyers operate and connect with their audience. In this chapter, we'll explore the transformative impact of social media on personal injury law practice and how you can leverage it to elevate your practice.

1. Client Acquisition in the Digital Age:

    In the era of smartphones and social networks, the journey of a potential client often begins online. Through your short form videos, potential clients can get a glimpse of your expertise, understand your values, and hear about successful cases, all before even setting foot in your office. This initial digital touchpoint not only expands your reach but also allows clients to make informed decisions about choosing you as their advocate.

2. Democratizing Legal Information:

Social media has made it possible to break down complex legal concepts into accessible, digestible content. By creating short form videos that explain legal rights, discuss common personal injury issues, or provide advice, you're not just showcasing your knowledge but also empowering your audience with valuable information. This democratization of legal information fosters a more informed and engaged community.

3. Building Trust and Credibility:

In the realm of personal injury law, trust and credibility are paramount. Social media allows you to build these attributes over time through consistent, valuable, and authentic content. By showcasing your successful cases, sharing client testimonials, or addressing questions and concerns, you're not just building a social media following; you're cultivating a community that trusts and values your expertise.

4. Showcasing the Human Side of Law:

Behind the legal jargon, the court hearings, and the case files, law is fundamentally about people. It's about their stories, their struggles, and their pursuit of justice. Social media gives you the platform to tell these stories, to show the human side of your practice, and to reinforce your commitment to your clients. This emotional connection can significantly enhance your brand image and client relationships.

5. Fostering Engagement and Dialogue:

The interactive nature of social media provides a unique opportunity to foster engagement and dialogue. You can respond to comments, address queries, or even host live Q&A sessions. This two-way communication can not only enhance your client relationships but also provide you with valuable insights into your audience's concerns and needs.

6. Strengthening Your Brand Identity:

As we've discussed in the previous chapter, social media is a powerful tool for building your brand identity. Your short form videos are like digital brushstrokes, each one contributing to the overall picture of your brand. Through strategic and consistent content, you can shape how your audience perceives your practice, reinforcing your values, mission, and unique selling propositions.

The impact of social media on the practice of personal injury law cannot be overstated. It has fundamentally altered the way lawyers connect with their audience, present their cases, and build their brands. However, this digital revolution is not without challenges. Ethical considerations, privacy concerns, and the constant need for content creation require careful navigation.

7. **Enhancing Case Presentation:**

Social media and short form videos offer an innovative way to present your cases. They allow you to distill complex legal issues into compelling narratives, supplemented by visuals, animations, or infographics. Whether it's a brief overview of a successful case or a series of videos explaining a complex lawsuit, these digital tools can amplify your case presentation skills and make legal intricacies more understandable to your audience.

8. **Expanding Professional Networks:**

While social media can connect you with potential clients, it can also help you build a robust professional network. Engaging with other lawyers, industry experts, or legal organizations can open up opportunities for collaborations, partnerships, or mentorships. Sharing or commenting on relevant content can position you as a thought leader in your field and expand your professional influence.

9. **Advocating for Justice:**

Social media provides a platform to advocate for justice outside the courtroom. You can raise awareness about legal rights, discuss societal issues related to personal injury law, or champion legal reforms. These advocacy efforts can reinforce your commitment to justice and elevate your stature from a personal injury lawyer to a crusader for clients' rights.

10. Managing Online Reputation:

In the digital world, your reputation is often shaped by your online presence. A well-managed social media platform that regularly posts valuable content and engages with its audience can boost your online reputation. Conversely, negative comments or reviews need to be addressed promptly and professionally to maintain your digital reputation.

11. Staying Updated and Relevant:

The legal landscape, like the digital world, is constantly evolving. Social media can keep you updated on the latest legal trends, changes in laws, or notable verdicts. It can also provide insights into trending topics or concerns among your audience, helping you stay relevant in your practice.

The digital revolution in the legal profession is here to stay, and it's continually evolving. By understanding and embracing the transformative impact of social media, personal injury lawyers can redefine their practice, extend their influence, and make justice more accessible and understandable to their audience.

In the chapters to follow, we will delve deeper into specific strategies for creating compelling short form videos, addressing digital challenges, and leveraging social media analytics. As we navigate through this exciting digital landscape, remember that the power of social media lies not just in its reach but in its ability to connect, engage, and inspire.

Chapter 7

Legal Edutainment: Informing, Educating, and Entertaining in Seconds

In a world teeming with information, capturing attention can be as challenging as catching smoke with your bare hands. Yet, that's the reality of social media marketing. Amidst the noise and distractions, how can you make your voice heard, your message understood, and your brand remembered? The answer lies in the magic of 'edutainment'.

Edutainment, a blend of education and entertainment, is a powerful content strategy that combines the informative value of education with the captivating appeal of entertainment. It's not about watering down legal information into trivial tidbits, but about presenting it in a way that's engaging, relatable, and memorable. As we navigate the realm of short form videos, let's explore how you can master the art of legal edutainment.

1. Know Your Audience:

    The first rule of edutainment is to know your audience. Understand their demographics, their interests, their concerns, and their language. This understanding will guide you in creating content that resonates with them, answers their questions, and speaks to their needs.

2. **Simplify, Don't Dumb Down:**

Legal concepts can be complex and intimidating for the layperson. Your goal is to simplify these concepts, not dumb them down. Use clear, straightforward language, but don't shy away from explaining legal terms or concepts. Your audience will appreciate your respect for their intelligence and your effort to empower them with knowledge.

3. **Use Storytelling Techniques:**

Stories are the lifeblood of edutainment. They draw people in, stir their emotions, and engrave your message in their memory. Whether it's a client success story, a fictional case scenario, or a narrative of a landmark verdict, infuse your videos with the power of storytelling.

4. **Harness the Power of Visuals:**

Short form videos provide a unique opportunity to translate words into visuals. Use infographics to explain legal processes, animations to illustrate case scenarios, or imagery to evoke emotions. Well-designed visuals not only enhance understanding but also make your videos more enjoyable.

5. **Inject Humor:**

Humor is a potent ingredient of edutainment. It breaks down barriers, lightens heavy topics, and makes learning enjoyable.

Incorporate humor into your videos through witty narration, amusing animations, or funny anecdotes. But remember, humor should never undermine the seriousness of legal issues or the respect for your profession.

6. Foster Engagement:

Edutainment is not a one-way street. Encourage your audience to interact with your content. Pose questions, invite opinions, or host quizzes. Engagement not only enriches the learning experience but also strengthens your connection with your audience.

7. Be Consistent and Relevant:

Consistency and relevance are crucial for successful edutainment. Ensure your content is consistently high-quality, informative, and entertaining. Stay relevant by addressing current legal issues, trending topics, or audience concerns.

8. Add a Personal Touch:

Adding a personal touch to your videos can enhance their relatability and appeal. Share your experiences, insights, or reflections. Show your audience the person behind the lawyer, the human behind the professional facade.

9. Call to Action:

Every piece of edutainment content should have a clear call to action. Whether it's inviting your audience to ask questions, encouraging them to share your video, or prompting them to reach out for a consultation, a call to action guides your audience on what to do next.

Legal edutainment is not just about producing entertaining videos; it's about redefining how legal information is perceived, understood, and appreciated. It's about turning passive viewers into active learners, curious followers into informed clients, and virtual strangers into engaged community members. When done right, legal edutainment can position you as a trusted advisor, a valued educator, and a compelling storyteller.

10. Master the Art of Brevity:

Short form videos are, by their nature, brief. The art of condensing complex information into minutes or even seconds is a skill that requires practice. Start by identifying your key message, then build a concise script around it. Every word, image, and second counts in short form videos, so make sure each element adds value to your message.

11. Reflect Your Brand:

Even within the realm of edutainment, your brand's voice should be clear and consistent. Your videos are an extension of your practice and should reflect your brand's personality, values, and promise. This consistency strengthens brand recognition and trust among your audience.

12. Leverage Social Media Features:

Email me directly at mike@mikekruzich.com if you would like me to personally assess your Lawfirm's social media presence

30

Each social media platform offers unique features that can enhance your edutainment content. From Instagram's reels and stickers to Twitter's polls and threads, familiarize yourself with these features and use them to make your videos more engaging and interactive.

13. Monitor Feedback and Adapt:

Edutainment is a dynamic process. Monitor your audience's responses, feedback, and engagement levels. What type of content are they most responsive to? What topics are they interested in? Use these insights to adapt your strategy, improve your content, and better serve your audience.

The beauty of legal edutainment lies in its ability to change the narrative of law from intimidating to inviting, from complex to comprehensible, and from dry to dynamic. By mastering the art of legal edutainment, you're not just creating entertaining videos; you're democratizing legal knowledge, empowering your audience, and transforming your practice in the process.

As we move forward to the next chapters, we'll delve deeper into the specific strategies for creating various types of short form videos, from explainer videos and case study videos to Q&A videos and behind-the-scenes videos. Through each type, we'll explore how to inform, educate, and entertain in seconds, and in the process, leave a lasting impact. The journey of legal edutainment is as exciting as it is rewarding, so let's dive in, one short form video at a time.

Chapter 8

Understanding Social Algorithms: Maximizing Reach and Engagement

Algorithms can be daunting. They're these mysterious, complex formulas that dictate the life and death of our content on social media platforms. Yet, understanding them is crucial to maximizing the reach and engagement of your short form videos. While each social media platform has its unique algorithm, several universal principles can guide you in navigating this algorithmic maze.

1. Quality over Quantity:

   Social media algorithms prioritize quality content. They assess quality based on factors such as engagement levels, viewing duration, and user feedback. So, focus on producing high-quality videos that provide value to your audience, provoke thought, and invite interaction.

   Let's take the example of Sarah, a personal injury lawyer who started posting short form videos on her firm's social media platforms. At first, Sarah was posting several videos each day, covering a wide range of legal topics. However, she noticed that her videos were getting minimal views and engagement.

   She decided to change her strategy. She reduced the number of videos she posted each week and focused on improving the quality of each video. She invested in better production equipment, spent more time researching and scripting each video, and began soliciting feedback from her followers to continually improve her content.

This change in strategy led to a significant improvement in the performance of her videos. Her views increased, her engagement rates skyrocketed, and she started gaining more followers. This story illustrates the importance of quality over quantity when it comes to social media content.

2. Consistency is Key:

Algorithms favor consistency. Regular posting signals to the algorithm that you're an active and reliable content producer. Establish a consistent posting schedule that suits your capacity and your audience's preferences.

3. Engage with Your Audience:

Algorithms love engagement. Likes, comments, shares, saves - these are all signals to the algorithm that your content is valuable and should be shown to more users. So, foster engagement by creating interactive content, responding to comments, and encouraging your audience to engage with your posts.

4. Utilize All Platform Features:

Social media platforms want you to use all their features. Whether it's Instagram's reels and IGTV or LinkedIn's polls and articles, utilizing these features can boost your content's visibility.

5. Understand User Behavior:

Algorithms aim to deliver content that users will enjoy and engage with. By understanding your audience's behavior, including their active hours, content preferences, and interaction patterns, you can align your content strategy with their behavior and boost your content's performance.

6. Experiment and Adapt:

Finally, remember that algorithms evolve. What works today may not work tomorrow. Stay updated on algorithm changes, experiment with different strategies, monitor your performance, and adapt accordingly.

Understanding social media algorithms is not about gaming the system or finding a magic formula. It's about aligning your content strategy with the goal of these algorithms - to deliver valuable, engaging, and enjoyable content to users. By focusing on quality, consistency, engagement, and adaptation, you can maximize your reach and engagement, and make your mark in the vast social media universe.

As we delve deeper into the world of short form videos in the upcoming chapters, keep these principles in mind. Remember, algorithms are not the enemy. They're simply tools that can help you connect with your audience, amplify your voice, and make a difference with your content.

7. The Impact of Video Performance Metrics:

    Performance metrics such as view duration, click-through rate, and completion rate play a critical role in how algorithms perceive the value of your content. For example, if your short form videos are frequently watched in their entirety, the algorithm takes it as a positive signal of user satisfaction and is likely to promote your content more.

8. Tailoring Content to the Platform:

    Each social media platform has its unique algorithm and audience. What works on Facebook might not work on TikTok or LinkedIn. Understanding the nuances of each platform and tailoring your content accordingly can significantly boost your visibility and engagement.

9. The Power of Shares and Saves:

    Shares and saves are particularly powerful engagement signals for algorithms. They indicate that your content is not just interesting but valuable enough for users to want to share with others or save for later. Encouraging such actions can elevate your standing in the eyes of the algorithm.

10. Algorithm-friendly Content Ideas:

Certain types of content tend to perform well algorithmically. How-to videos, Q&A sessions, behind-the-scenes glimpses, and user-generated content are some examples. Experiment with different content types and formats to discover what resonates most with your audience and the algorithm.

11. The Role of Hashtags and Keywords:

Hashtags and keywords help algorithms categorize your content and serve it to users interested in those topics. Using relevant, specific, and trending hashtags and keywords can increase your content's discoverability.

Let's consider the case of John, another personal injury lawyer who was new to social media. John was producing high-quality content, but he was struggling to get his videos seen. He realized he had been neglecting the power of keywords and hashtags. He started researching trending legal hashtags and popular legal keywords, incorporating them into his video descriptions and titles.

He also used hashtags to participate in trending discussions relevant to his field. This not only boosted his visibility but also positioned him as a part of the larger conversation happening in the legal community. John's story underscores the importance of effective keyword and hashtag usage in enhancing the reach of your content.

Understanding and navigating the world of social media algorithms can feel like decoding a complex puzzle. But once you recognize their underlying logic and purpose – to maximize user satisfaction and engagement – you can start to turn them into your allies rather than adversaries. They can become powerful tools in your strategy, helping you connect more effectively with your audience and amplify your impact. With the insights from this chapter, you're now better equipped to take on the algorithms and let your content shine in the vast digital landscape of social media.

Chapter 9

Adapting to Different Platforms: TikTok, Instagram Reels, and Beyond

The social media landscape is diverse and ever-changing. Each platform has its unique characteristics, audience, and possibilities. As a personal injury lawyer, understanding these differences and knowing how to adapt your short form video content to each platform is a crucial skill. In this chapter, we'll explore some of the most popular platforms for short form videos - TikTok and Instagram Reels - and discuss strategies for maximizing your impact on these platforms and beyond.

1. Understanding TikTok:

    TikTok is the birthplace of the short form video revolution. With its young, engaged audience and creative, unpredictable content, TikTok offers immense potential for personal injury lawyers willing to embrace its playful, authentic vibe.

    A key factor to consider when creating content for TikTok is its audience. TikTok users are primarily Gen Z and young millennials, which means they appreciate authenticity, creativity, and social consciousness. The algorithm also heavily favors engagement and completion rate, so creating captivating, shareable content is a must.

Email me directly at mike@mikekruzich.com if you would like me to personally assess your Lawfirm's social media presence.

39

An excellent example of this is a personal injury lawyer named Emily. Emily understood the TikTok landscape and created a series of short, catchy videos explaining common legal terms and processes in simple language. She used humor, popular music, and trending formats to make her videos engaging and relatable. Her videos were a hit, gaining thousands of views and shares, proving that legal content can indeed thrive in the vibrant world of TikTok.

2. Mastering Instagram Reels:

    Instagram Reels is Instagram's answer to TikTok. It offers similar features but operates within the Instagram ecosystem, giving you access to Instagram's diverse audience. Instagram Reels is perfect for visually appealing, concise, and creative content.

    The Instagram audience is broader than TikTok's, spanning various age groups and interests. Therefore, a more diverse content strategy can work well here. Instagram's algorithm favors content that receives high engagement, especially within the first few hours of posting, so timely engagement with your audience is crucial.

    Take the case of David, a personal injury lawyer who leveraged Instagram Reels to showcase client testimonials and success stories. He created visually compelling, emotionally resonant short videos featuring his clients sharing their experiences.

These videos garnered high engagement and helped build trust and credibility for David's practice.

3. Exploring Other Platforms:

   While TikTok and Instagram Reels dominate the short form video scene, other platforms like Snapchat, LinkedIn, and Facebook also offer short form video features. Snapchat is great for casual, candid content, LinkedIn favors professional and educational content, while Facebook's vast user base provides a broader audience.

4. Adapting Content Across Platforms:

   While creating unique content for each platform is ideal, it's not always feasible. An effective strategy can be to create a core piece of content and then adapt it to each platform. This means adjusting the format, tone, length, and other elements to suit each platform's requirements and audience.

   For example, you could create a detailed explanation video for LinkedIn, then trim it down to a catchy, quick-tip video for TikTok, and a visually appealing infographic video for Instagram Reels. This approach allows you to maximize your content's reach without overstretching your resources.

5. Staying Updated:

Social media is constantly evolving, with new platforms, features, and trends emerging all the time. Stay updated on these changes, experiment with new platforms and features, and be ready to adapt your strategy as needed.

In conclusion, mastering different social media platforms requires understanding each platform's unique characteristics and audience and adapting your content and strategy accordingly. The beauty of social media is its diversity - each platform offers unique ways to connect with different audiences & share your message.

6. Leveraging Platform-Specific Features:

Each platform comes with specific features designed to enhance user engagement. On TikTok, you can tap into trending challenges or use popular soundtracks to increase your content's visibility. Instagram Reels allows you to leverage the power of hashtags and the Explore page. On LinkedIn, you can participate in relevant industry groups and use professional hashtags to expand your reach. Understanding and effectively using these features can significantly boost your content's performance.

7. Building a Consistent Brand Identity Across Platforms:

While the tone and format of your content may vary across platforms, maintaining a consistent brand identity is crucial. Your brand identity includes your brand message, values, visual elements, and overall personality. A consistent brand identity makes you easily recognizable across platforms and helps build trust and loyalty among your audience.

Consider Jennifer, a personal injury lawyer who has created a strong brand identity as a compassionate, determined advocate for her clients. Regardless of the platform, whether she's sharing a client story on Instagram Reels, explaining a legal concept on TikTok, or sharing industry insights on LinkedIn, Jennifer maintains her brand identity. This consistency has not only made her instantly recognizable across platforms but has also helped her build a loyal, engaged follower base.

8. Analytics and Performance Tracking:

    Each platform provides analytics tools that allow you to track your content's performance, understand your audience behavior, and gain insights into what works and what doesn't. Regularly reviewing and analyzing these metrics can help you refine your strategy, improve your content, and increase your impact.

9. Engaging with Your Audience:

    Engaging with your audience is crucial, no matter the platform. Respond to comments, ask for feedback, host Q&A sessions, and show appreciation for your followers. This not only fosters a sense of community but also boosts your content's visibility by increasing engagement.

10. Balancing Promotion and Value:

While promoting your services is important, constantly bombarding your audience with promotional content can be off-putting. Aim for a balance between promotional and value-adding content. This could be educational content, behind-the-scenes glimpses, personal stories, or content that entertains or inspires.

The key to successfully adapting to different platforms lies in understanding the unique characteristics of each platform, creating and adapting content to suit each platform, and maintaining a consistent brand identity. With these strategies, you can maximize your reach, engage effectively with your audience, and harness the power of short form videos to enhance your personal injury law practice. Remember, social media is not a one-size-fits-all game. Embrace its diversity, stay adaptable, and let your authenticity shine, no matter the platform.

Chapter 10

Short Form Video Analytics: Interpreting Data to Improve Your Strategy

As you delve deeper into the world of social media, you'll soon realize that data is your best ally. Social media platforms provide a wealth of information about how your content is performing and how your audience is engaging with it. Understanding this data, commonly referred to as analytics, is critical to refining your strategy, improving your content, and growing your impact. In this chapter, we'll explore the most important short form video analytics and how to interpret them to enhance your social media strategy.

1. Understanding Views and Impressions:

    Views and impressions are the most basic metrics, representing how many times your video has been watched or appeared in a user's feed. These metrics give you a sense of your content's reach but remember, not all views are equal. Completion rate, or the percentage of viewers who watch your video till the end, is a more accurate indicator of your content's effectiveness.

    Consider the story of Richard, a personal injury lawyer who was initially thrilled to see his videos getting thousands of views. However, upon closer inspection, he realized that most viewers were dropping off within the first few seconds. This prompted Richard to revise his video introductions, making them more engaging and instantly captivating. His video completion rates improved significantly, leading to better overall performance.

2. Engagement Metrics: Likes, Shares, Comments, and Saves:

Engagement metrics measure how users interact with your content. Likes, shares, comments, and saves are all strong indicators of how much your audience values your content. High engagement often translates to higher visibility in the algorithm, leading to a wider reach.

3. Audience Demographics and Behavior:

Understanding who your audience is and how they behave is critical to tailoring your content and strategy. Metrics like age, gender, location, peak activity times, and most-watched content can provide valuable insights into your audience's preferences and behavior.

4. Click-Through Rate (CTR):

CTR is the percentage of viewers who clicked on your call-to-action or profile link after watching your video. A high CTR indicates that your content is compelling enough to drive viewers to take the desired action, such as visiting your website or learning more about your services.

5. Follower Growth Rate:

This metric shows how quickly you're gaining new followers. While rapid follower growth can be exciting, remember that quality trumps quantity. It's better to have a smaller, engaged audience that values your content than a large, uninterested one.

6. Video Shares and Saves:

Video shares and saves are strong indicators of high-quality content. When a viewer shares your video with their followers or saves it for later, it shows that they found your content valuable and worth revisiting or sharing.

7. Top Performing Content:

Analyzing your top performing content can provide insights into what types of content resonate most with your audience. Look for patterns in your most successful videos - do they have a common theme, format, or style? Use these insights to guide your future content creation.

8. Experiment and Learn:

Don't be afraid to experiment with different types of content, formats, and strategies. Use analytics to evaluate the success of your experiments and learn from the results. Remember, what works for one lawyer or audience may not work for you. Stay open, adaptable, and always be learning.

9. Long-Term Trends:

While it's important to stay responsive to short-term metrics and trends, don't lose sight of the bigger picture. Track your metrics over time to identify long-term trends and patterns. This can help you understand your overall growth trajectory and evaluate the long-term success of your strategy.

To sum up, analytics provide a wealth of insights into your content's performance, your audience's behavior, and the effectiveness of your strategy. They help you understand what's working, what's not, and how you can improve. Remember, data is just a tool. It's how you interpret and act upon it that makes the difference.

Consider the case of Laura, a personal injury lawyer who, after noticing a drop in her engagement rates, decided to delve into her analytics. She found that her videos were primarily being viewed late in the evening, while she was posting them early in the morning. By simply adjusting her posting schedule to match her audience's peak activity times, she saw a significant increase in engagement.

10. Leveraging Tools and Resources:

There are numerous tools and resources available to help you track, analyze, and interpret your social media analytics. From in-app analytics tools provided by the platforms themselves to third-party analytics tools that offer more detailed insights, choose the tools that best fit your needs and capabilities.

Email me directly at mike@mikekruzich.com if you would like me to personally assess your Lawfirm's social media presence

48

11. Making Data-Driven Decisions:

The insights you gain from analytics should form the basis of your decision-making. Whether it's deciding what content to create, when to post it, or how to engage with your audience, let your data guide you. This doesn't mean you should ignore your intuition or creativity - rather, it means combining these elements with hard data to make informed, effective decisions.

12. The Power of Incremental Improvements:

Remember, improving your social media performance is a marathon, not a sprint. Small, incremental improvements, consistently implemented, can lead to significant growth over time. Celebrate your wins, learn from your failures, and keep striving to improve.

In conclusion, mastering short form video analytics is a crucial skill for any personal injury lawyer looking to enhance their social media strategy. It allows you to understand your audience, improve your content, and grow your impact. So embrace the numbers, delve into the data, and let your analytics illuminate the path to social media success.

Chapter 11

Authenticity and Consistency: The Key to Social Media Longevity

In the fast-paced, ever-evolving world of social media, maintaining your audience's attention and loyalty can be challenging. Trends come and go, algorithms change, and new platforms emerge. However, two elements remain evergreen in their ability to create a strong, enduring social media presence: authenticity and consistency. In this chapter, we'll explore why these elements are so critical and how you can harness them to achieve social media longevity.

1. Understanding Authenticity:

    Authenticity is about being genuine and real. It's about showing up as your true self, sharing your unique perspective, and being honest and transparent with your audience. Authenticity builds trust and connection, making your audience feel seen, heard, and valued.

    Consider the story of Alan, a personal injury lawyer who used to post polished, formal videos on social media. While his videos were professional, they failed to resonate with his audience. He decided to switch things up, sharing more about his personal experiences, challenges, and learnings in the field of personal injury law. His videos became more relatable and engaging, and his audience responded positively to his authenticity.

2. The Power of Consistency:

Consistency is not just about posting regularly, although that is important. It's also about maintaining a consistent tone, message, and brand identity across your content and platforms. Consistency helps your audience know what to expect from you, creating a sense of familiarity and reliability.

3. The Intersection of Authenticity and Consistency:

When authenticity and consistency intersect, they create a strong, distinctive brand identity. This brand identity becomes your signature, making you recognizable and memorable in the crowded social media landscape.

4. Authenticity in Action:

Being authentic doesn't mean you have to share every detail of your life or stray from your professional image. It means being true to your values, your mission, and your audience. Share your passion for personal injury law, your commitment to your clients, and your insights and experiences in a way that's true to you.

5. Consistency in Action:

Being consistent means showing up regularly for your audience, both in terms of frequency and quality. Develop a content calendar, establish a regular posting schedule, and stick to it. Ensure your content maintains a consistent level of quality, and stay true to your brand identity in every post.

6. Navigating the Balance:

    Balancing authenticity and consistency can be tricky. You might feel the pressure to keep up with trends or to present an image that's not entirely 'you'. Remember, while it's important to stay relevant and adaptable, never compromise your authenticity for the sake of consistency, or vice versa.

7. Long-Term Benefits of Authenticity and Consistency:

    Authenticity and consistency provide numerous long-term benefits. They build trust and loyalty with your audience, enhance your brand reputation, and increase your resilience amidst changes and challenges. They also foster a deeper connection with your audience, turning them from passive viewers into engaged followers and advocates.

8. Evolving Authentically:

    As you grow and evolve, both personally and professionally, so too will your social media presence. Authenticity is not a static state - it's a continuous journey of self-expression and connection. Stay open to growth and evolution, but always stay true to your core.

Email me directly at mike@mikekruzich.com if you would like me to personally assess your Lawfirm's social media presence

52

9. Staying Consistent Amidst Change:

    While it's important to stay adaptable and responsive to
    changes and trends, maintaining consistency amidst change is
    crucial. Whether it's a new social media platform, a change in
    the algorithm, or a shift in your audience's preferences, always
    stay true to your brand identity and your audience.

In conclusion, authenticity and consistency are the cornerstone of
a successful, enduring social media presence. They help you build a
strong, distinctive brand identity, foster trust and loyalty with your
audience, and navigate changes and challenges with resilience.
They turn your social media platforms from mere marketing tools
into platforms for connection, engagement, and impact.

Consider the story of Maya, a personal injury lawyer who built a
robust social media presence based on authenticity and consistency.
Despite changes in trends, algorithms, and platforms, her
commitment to being true to herself and her audience allowed her to
maintain a strong, engaged following over the years. Her story serves
as a reminder that while strategies, tools, and platforms may change,
the principles of authenticity and consistency remain timeless.

In the chapters to come, we'll delve deeper into specific strategies,
tools, and techniques to enhance your social media presence. But
remember, at the heart of all these strategies is the commitment to
showing up authentically and consistently for your audience. This

is the key to social media longevity and the foundation upon which all your other efforts rest.

Chapter 12

The Power of Testimonials: Humanizing Your Practice through Client Stories

One of the most powerful tools at your disposal as a personal injury lawyer using short form video on social media is the testimonial. Testimonials, or client stories, serve multiple purposes. They not only validate your professional abilities and successes, but they also humanize your practice. This chapter will delve into how testimonials can elevate your social media presence, make your content more relatable, and ultimately, create a deeper connection with your audience.

1. The Importance of Testimonials:

   Testimonials are personal stories from your clients sharing their experience working with you. They provide social proof, which is a psychological phenomenon where people follow the actions of others under the assumption that those actions are reflective of the correct behavior. In the context of personal injury law, when potential clients see that others have had positive experiences with your services, they are more likely to trust and consider you for their own needs.

2. Humanizing Your Practice:

   Testimonials humanize your practice by showcasing real people with real stories. They demonstrate the impact of your work on people's lives, making your practice more relatable and approachable.

Consider the story of Jonathan, a personal injury lawyer who started sharing client testimonials on his social media platforms. He noticed an immediate increase in engagement and enquiries, with many potential clients mentioning how the testimonials had resonated with them and made them feel more confident about choosing Jonathan for their legal needs.

3. Crafting Compelling Testimonials:

A compelling testimonial is authentic, relatable, and impactful. It highlights not just the outcome of the case, but also the client's journey, their challenges, and how your services helped them. Remember, your audience is not just interested in the end result, but also the process - how you communicate, how you handle challenges, and how you support your clients through difficult times.

4. Video Testimonials:

Video testimonials are particularly powerful. They allow your audience to see your clients' emotions, hear their tone, and feel a deeper connection to their stories. Consider investing in high-quality video testimonials to enhance their impact.

5. Legal and Ethical Considerations:

Before sharing a client testimonial, it's important to obtain your client's consent and ensure that you're respecting their privacy and confidentiality. Be aware of the legal and ethical guidelines in your jurisdiction and abide by them at all times.

6. Incorporating Testimonials into Your Content Strategy:

   Testimonials should be a key part of your content strategy. They can be shared as standalone videos, incorporated into informational content, or used to highlight specific aspects of your services. Be creative and strategic in how you use testimonials to amplify your message and humanize your practice.

7. Responding to Testimonials:

   When you share a testimonial, take the time to respond to comments and engage with your audience. This not only fosters a deeper connection with your audience, but also demonstrates your commitment to your clients and your appreciation for their stories.

8. Overcoming Challenges:

   Not all cases will have a positive outcome, and not all clients will have a positive experience. Be prepared for this, and consider how you can share these stories in a way that highlights your commitment to your clients and your dedication to your work, even when things don't go as planned.

In conclusion, testimonials are a powerful tool to humanize your practice, build trust with your audience, and showcase the impact of your work. They allow you to tell your story through the eyes of your clients, making your content more relatable, engaging, and impactful. As you delve deeper into the world of short form video and social media, remember to leverage the power of testimonials to elevate your practice and connect with your audience.

Chapter 13

Behind the Scenes: Showcasing Your Team and Your Process

In the world of personal injury law, building trust and rapport with your clients is paramount. One highly effective way to achieve this, particularly in the realm of short-form video for social media, is by giving your audience a behind-the-scenes look at your team and your process. This chapter will discuss how showcasing your team and your process can enhance transparency, foster connection, and ultimately, set you apart in the competitive landscape of personal injury law.

1. The Power of Transparency:

   Transparency is a key component of trust. By giving your audience a glimpse into your day-to-day operations, you're showing them that you have nothing to hide. This builds trust and enhances your reputation as an open, honest law practice.

2. Showcasing Your Team:

   Your team is your greatest asset. By showcasing your team, you humanize your practice, making it more relatable and approachable. Share videos introducing your team members, highlighting their skills and experiences, and showcasing their personalities. This not only highlights the collective expertise of your practice but also demonstrates the people behind the work, fostering a deeper connection with your audience.

Consider the story of Sandra, a personal injury lawyer who started sharing 'Meet the Team' videos on her social media platforms. Her audience loved getting to know the individuals behind the practice, and it created a sense of familiarity and trust that significantly boosted her engagement and client inquiries.

3. Showcasing Your Process:

   Giving your audience a glimpse into your process helps demystify the legal process and gives them a better understanding of what to expect when working with you. Share videos showing how you approach cases, how you communicate with clients, and how you navigate challenges. Make sure to break down complex legal jargon into simple, understandable language.

4. Making it Engaging:

   While behind-the-scenes content is valuable, it's important to present it in a way that's engaging and interesting. Keep your videos short, dynamic, and personable. Use storytelling techniques to make your content more compelling and memorable.

5. Balancing Professionalism and Personality:

   While it's important to showcase your team and your process, it's equally important to maintain a level of professionalism.

Balance showcasing your personality with maintaining the professional image that's expected in the field of law.

6. Respecting Privacy and Confidentiality:

   While sharing behind-the-scenes content, it's crucial to respect the privacy and confidentiality of your clients and your cases. Always get necessary permissions and ensure you're not revealing any sensitive or confidential information.

7. Consistency is Key:

   Just like with any other aspect of your social media strategy, consistency is key when it comes to sharing behind-the-scenes content. Regularly update your audience about your team and your process, and make it a consistent part of your content strategy.

In conclusion, showcasing your team and your process through behind-the-scenes content is a powerful way to build trust, foster connection, and humanize your practice. It allows your audience to see the people and the work behind your success, creating a deeper sense of familiarity and trust. So, don't be afraid to pull back the curtain and let your audience in. The authenticity and transparency you demonstrate will only serve to elevate your practice in the eyes of your audience.

Chapter 14

The Art of Collaboration: Leveraging Influencers and Partnerships in the Legal Field

In the expansive universe of social media, the power of collaboration cannot be underestimated. By connecting with influencers and forming strategic partnerships, you can significantly extend your reach, enhance your credibility, and bring fresh, dynamic content to your audience. This chapter will explore the art of collaboration in the legal field, and how you, as a personal injury lawyer, can effectively leverage influencers and partnerships in your social media strategy.

1. Understanding the Power of Collaboration:

    Collaboration, when executed correctly, is a win-win situation. You benefit from the extended reach and influence of your collaborator, while they gain access to your audience and expertise. It can lead to cross-promotion, mutual growth, and increased engagement.

2. Identifying Potential Collaborators:

    The first step in leveraging collaboration is identifying potential collaborators. Look for influencers and organizations that align with your values, have a significant presence in your target demographic, and can bring value to your audience.

3. Influencers in the Legal Field:

   While the concept of influencers is typically associated with fields like fashion, beauty, or fitness, there is a growing number of influencers in the legal field. These are individuals who have built a strong online following based on their legal expertise and insights. Collaborating with these influencers can bring credibility and visibility to your practice.

   Consider the story of Alex, a personal injury lawyer who collaborated with a popular legal influencer for a series of short-form videos on personal injury law. The collaboration significantly increased Alex's visibility and brought him a surge of new clients.

4. Forming Strategic Partnerships:

   Partnerships extend beyond individual influencers to include other law firms, legal organizations, or even non-legal entities. For example, a partnership with a healthcare provider could provide valuable content for your audience around medical issues related to personal injury cases.

5. Navigating Collaboration Agreements:

   When entering into a collaboration, it's crucial to have a clear agreement in place. This should outline the expectations, responsibilities, and terms of the collaboration. Remember, as a lawyer, your reputation and credibility are paramount, so ensure any collaborations align with your professional standards.

6. Creating Collaborative Content:

   Collaborative content should be a blend of both parties' expertise and perspectives. This could take the form of joint videos, interviews, Q&A sessions, or shared case studies. Be creative and think about what would provide the most value and interest for your audience.

7. Promoting Collaborative Content:

   Promotion is key in any collaboration. Ensure both parties actively promote the collaborative content to their audiences. This could be through social media posts, email newsletters, or even personal messages.

8. Evaluating the Success of Collaborations:

   After a collaboration, take the time to evaluate its success. Look at metrics like engagement, audience growth, and client inquiries. Use these insights to refine your collaboration strategy moving forward.

In conclusion, collaboration is a powerful tool in your social media strategy. By leveraging influencers and partnerships, you can extend your reach, enhance your credibility, and provide dynamic, varied content for your audience. As you continue to navigate the world of short-form video and social media, remember to consider the power of collaboration in advancing your practice and making a larger impact in your field.

Chapter 15

Legal Jargon, Simplified: Making Law Understandable to the Masses

In the realm of personal injury law, complex legal jargon is often a barrier to understanding for many clients. As a lawyer utilizing short-form video on social media, one of your key responsibilities is to break down these complexities into easily digestible content. This chapter will discuss the importance of simplifying legal jargon and provide tips and techniques to effectively communicate legal concepts to a lay audience.

1. The Importance of Simplifying Legal Jargon:

    Legal jargon, while essential within the legal profession, can often be confusing and intimidating for clients. By simplifying this jargon, you make your content more accessible, increase understanding, and foster trust with your audience.

2. Understanding Your Audience:

    The first step to simplifying legal jargon is understanding your audience. Who are they? What is their level of understanding of legal concepts? The answers to these questions will guide your content creation process.

3. **Breaking Down Complex Concepts:**

When communicating complex legal concepts, aim to break them down into smaller, understandable parts. Use simple, clear language, and avoid unnecessary legal terminology.

4. **Using Analogies and Metaphors:**

Analogies and metaphors can be powerful tools in making complex concepts more understandable. By relating unfamiliar legal concepts to familiar everyday experiences, you can significantly enhance understanding.

Consider the story of Maria, a personal injury lawyer who used the metaphor of a football game to explain the process of a lawsuit. This creative approach not only made the content more understandable but also more engaging, leading to a significant increase in her video engagement.

5. **Visual Aids:**

Visual aids can significantly enhance understanding and retention of information. Consider using graphics, animations, or even props to illustrate your points.

6. **Creating a Series:**

Sometimes, a single video isn't enough to fully explain a complex legal concept. Consider creating a series of short videos, each tackling a different aspect of the concept. This allows you to delve deeper into each aspect without overwhelming your audience.

7. Encouraging Questions:

Encourage your audience to ask questions. This not only promotes engagement but also provides you with valuable insights into what aspects your audience finds confusing, allowing you to further tailor your content.

8. Staying Accurate:

While simplifying legal jargon is important, accuracy is paramount. Ensure that in your efforts to simplify, you don't misrepresent or oversimplify to the point of inaccuracy.

9. Regularly Updating Your Content:

Laws and regulations change regularly. Ensure your content is regularly updated to reflect these changes and provide the most accurate and relevant information to your audience.

In conclusion, as a personal injury lawyer in the realm of short-form video, simplifying legal jargon is a key component of your role. By making complex legal concepts more accessible, you can foster trust, enhance understanding, and ultimately, provide better service to your clients. So, embrace the challenge of simplification, and remember, in the words of Albert Einstein, "If you can't explain it simply, you don't understand it well enough."

Chapter 16

Harnessing Emotion: Telling Compelling Stories that Resonate

Storytelling has been a cornerstone of human communication since time immemorial. From Jesus Christ's parables to Walt Disney's enchanting narratives, the most influential figures in history understood the power of storytelling to captivate audiences, transmit values, and inspire action. This chapter will explore the art of storytelling in the context of short-form videos for personal injury lawyers, focusing on how you can harness emotion to tell compelling stories that resonate with your audience.

1. The Power of Storytelling:

    Stories have the unique ability to touch our hearts, stir our emotions, and create a lasting impact. They make complex concepts more relatable, create a sense of connection, and serve as a powerful tool for persuasion and influence.

2. Emotion as a Storytelling Tool:

    Emotion is a fundamental element of storytelling. By tapping into your audience's emotions, you can create a deeper connection, foster empathy, and inspire action. Remember, people may forget what you said, but they'll never forget how you made them feel.

Email me directly at mike@mikekruzich.com if you would like me to personally assess your Lawfirm's social media presence.

70

3. Learning from the Masters:

Some of the greatest storytellers in history have effectively harnessed the power of emotion. Take Jesus Christ, for example. His parables, or simple stories used to illustrate a moral or spiritual lesson, used familiar scenarios and relatable characters to evoke emotion and convey profound truths. The stories were simple yet powerful, and they have resonated with millions of people over the centuries.

Similarly, Walt Disney understood the power of emotional storytelling. His enchanting tales, filled with love, adventure, triumph, and loss, captivate audiences by touching their hearts and stirring their emotions. Despite being animations, Disney's stories feel incredibly human, highlighting universal experiences and emotions that resonate with viewers of all ages.

4. Crafting Emotional Stories:

The first step in crafting an emotional story is understanding your audience. What are their fears, hopes, and dreams? What challenges are they facing? Use this understanding to craft stories that reflect their experiences and emotions.

5. Show, Don't Tell:

In storytelling, showing is far more powerful than telling. Instead of simply stating facts, show them through actions, experiences, and emotions. This not only makes your story more engaging but also allows your audience to draw their own conclusions, leading to a deeper understanding and connection.

6. Authenticity is Key:

Authenticity is crucial in emotional storytelling. Audiences can tell when emotions are forced or fake, and it can damage your credibility. Share real experiences and genuine emotions to create authentic, impactful stories.

Consider the story of David, a personal injury lawyer who shared a personal story about a family member who had been a victim of a personal injury case. His genuine emotion and personal connection to the story resonated deeply with his audience, leading to a significant increase in engagement and client inquiries.

7. Balancing Emotion and Professionalism:

While emotion is a powerful tool, it's important to balance it with professionalism. You are a lawyer, and while emotional stories can create a connection with your audience, you should also maintain a level of professionalism and credibility.

8. Ending with a Call to Action:

Every story should have a purpose, and in the context of personal injury law, this is often a call to action. Whether it's encouraging viewers to seek legal advice, take safety precautions, or simply empathize with the victims of personal injury cases, make sure your story encourages your audience to take action.

9. Parasocial Bonding: The Next Frontier in Emotional Storytelling:

Parasocial interactions refer to the one-sided emotional bonds that audiences develop with media figures. In the world of social media, these bonds are increasingly common, and they offer a unique opportunity for personal injury lawyers to connect with their audience on a deeper level.

As a lawyer sharing content on social media, you're not just a face on a screen – you become a part of your audience's social network. They may feel like they know you personally, and this can create a strong emotional bond that enhances trust and loyalty.

By sharing personal stories, experiences, and emotions, you can foster parasocial bonding with your audience. These bonds can make your audience more receptive to your messages, encourage them to engage with your content, and ultimately, enhance your impact as a lawyer.

Remember, social media is a two-way street. Encourage your audience to share their own stories and experiences, respond to comments, and show appreciation for their support. This active engagement can further strengthen parasocial bonds and enhance your connection with your audience.

Take the case of Emma, a personal injury lawyer who regularly shares her day-to-day experiences as a lawyer and mother. Her authentic, relatable content has fostered a strong parasocial bond with her audience, leading to a high level of engagement and a loyal community of followers.

Harnessing emotion and fostering parasocial bonds can truly revolutionize the way personal injury lawyers connect with their audience on social media. By following the steps outlined in this chapter, you can use short-form videos to tell compelling stories that not only resonate with your audience but also foster deeper, more meaningful connections.

Chapter 17

Live Streaming: The Next Frontier in Social Media

Live streaming has rapidly grown in popularity, revolutionizing the way we consume and create content. With its real-time interaction and raw authenticity, it presents a unique opportunity for personal injury lawyers to connect with their audience on a deeper level. As someone who once held the title of the #1 most viewed TikTok live streamer, averaging over 1 million unique viewers on my live streams every day, I can attest to the immense power and potential of live streaming.

1. The Power of Live Streaming:

   Live streaming allows for real-time interaction, creating a sense of connection and immediacy that pre-recorded videos simply cannot match. It allows you to engage with your audience directly, answer their questions, and foster a sense of community.

2. My Experience as a Live Streamer:

   During my time as the #1 most viewed TikTok live streamer, I experienced firsthand the power of live streaming. The real-time interaction allowed me to connect with my audience on a deeper level, and the raw, unedited nature of the content made it feel more authentic and relatable. I found that people were not only more engaged during the live streams, but they were also more likely to follow up and engage with my subsequent content.

3. Platforms for Live Streaming:

    There are various platforms available for live streaming, each with its own strengths and weaknesses:

    - TikTok: Offers a large, engaged user base, especially among younger audiences. Its algorithm also provides excellent discoverability for new creators. However, it can be challenging to build a professional image on the platform due to its casual, entertainment-focused nature.

    - Facebook Live: Allows you to reach your existing network of Facebook friends or Page followers. Its robust advertising tools can also help you reach a larger audience. However, its user base tends to be older, which may not align with your target demographic.

    - YouTube Live: Known for its high-quality streams and long-form content. It also integrates well with Google's suite of tools. However, it can be challenging to get discovered as a new creator due to high competition.

    - Instagram Live: Great for reaching your existing Instagram followers and promoting your streams on your feed and stories. However, its discovery features are not as robust as TikTok or YouTube.

Email me directly at mike@mikekruzich.com if you would like me to personally assess your Lawfirm's social media presence

76

•

4. Multi-Streaming with Streamlabs:

Streamlabs is a streaming software that allows you to stream on multiple platforms at once. This can significantly increase your reach and save you time. However, it's important to consider the nuances of each platform and tailor your content and interaction accordingly.

5. Automating Live Streams:

I managed to automate my live streams by prerecording them and playing them in a loop 24/7 via Streamlabs. This allowed me to consistently engage with my audience, even when I was not physically present. However, it's important to strike a balance between live and automated content to maintain authenticity and real-time interaction.

6. Balancing Live Streaming and Short Form Videos:

While live streaming offers unique advantages, it should not replace short form videos entirely. Instead, they should complement each other as part of a balanced content strategy. For example, you can use short form videos to promote your live streams or follow up on topics discussed during the streams.

7. Legal Considerations for Live Streaming:

As a lawyer, it's crucial to consider the legal implications of live streaming. Always respect privacy laws, avoid making defamatory statements, and be careful not to provide legal advice that could be construed as establishing a lawyer-client relationship.

In conclusion, live streaming is a powerful tool that can enhance your short-form video strategy. By understanding the nuances of each platform, harnessing tools like Streamlabs, you can connect with your audience in a way that very few lawyers are.

Chapter 18

Mastering Video SEO: How to Make Your Content Discoverable

Search engine optimization (SEO) is a fundamental part of any online strategy, and video content is no exception. In the world of short-form videos, it's easy to overlook the importance of SEO, focusing instead on the virality factor. While viral videos can indeed bring significant reach, they tend to attract a broad and diverse audience. By contrast, SEO can help your content appear in search results and attract viewers who are actively interested in your field – the intent-based viewers.

1. Understanding Video SEO:

   Video SEO involves optimizing your videos to be indexed and rank on the search engine results pages for relevant keyword searches. This can include optimizing the video title, description, and tags, as well as leveraging platform-specific features like YouTube's video transcript feature.

2. Virality vs. Intent-Based Viewers:

   While viral videos can attract a large audience, they often appeal to a broad demographic, which may not necessarily be interested in personal injury law. By contrast, intent-based viewers are those who are actively searching for content related to your field. They are likely to be more engaged and potentially more valuable to your practice.

3. Keyword Research:

The first step in video SEO is to conduct keyword research. Identify the keywords that your target audience is likely to use when searching for content related to personal injury law. There are various tools available for this, such as Google's Keyword Planner and SEMRush.

4. Optimizing Video Titles and Descriptions:

Once you've identified your keywords, incorporate them into your video titles and descriptions. However, avoid keyword stuffing – the practice of overloading your content with keywords – as this can harm your SEO. Instead, strive for a natural incorporation of keywords into engaging and descriptive text.

5. Using Tags Wisely:

Tags are another critical component of video SEO. They help the platform's algorithm understand what your video is about and who might be interested in it. Use your keywords as tags, but also consider related terms and phrases that your audience might use.

6. Engaging Thumbnails and Captions:

Thumbnails and captions can significantly impact your video's click-through rate, which in turn can influence your video's search ranking. Design engaging thumbnails that accurately represent your video content and use captions to provide a brief overview of the video or to highlight intriguing points.

7. Utilizing Video Transcripts:

For platforms like YouTube, providing a video transcript can further boost your video SEO. Transcripts make your content accessible to a broader audience, including people with hearing impairments and those who prefer reading to watching videos. Plus, they allow the platform's algorithm to better understand your video content.

8. Encouraging Engagement:

The engagement that your video receives – likes, comments, shares, and watch time – can also influence its search ranking. Therefore, aim to create engaging content that prompts viewers to interact with your video.

9. Understanding Platform Algorithms:

Each social media platform has its own algorithm that determines which videos to display in search results and feeds. It's important to understand these algorithms and tailor your SEO strategy accordingly. For example, TikTok's algorithm appears to prioritize user engagement and relevance, while

YouTube's algorithm considers factors like relevance, engagement, and video quality.

10. Monitoring Your Performance:

Finally, use the analytics tools provided by each platform to monitor your video's performance and adjust your SEO strategy as needed. Look at metrics like views, engagement rate, and watch time, as well as where your traffic is coming from.

In conclusion, while the virality of short-form videos can provide a significant reach, video SEO is crucial for attracting intent-based viewers. By mastering video SEO, you can make your content discoverable and attract an audience that is actively interested in your field, thus potentially driving more meaningful engagement and conversions for your practice.

Chapter 19

Safeguarding Ethics in Social Media: The Fine Line Between Persuasion and Manipulation

As a personal injury lawyer, you strive to inform, educate, and advocate, using social media as a powerful tool to reach wider audiences. However, as we embrace these digital platforms, it's crucial to keep in mind the ethical considerations involved. Specifically, we must navigate the fine line between persuasion and manipulation, ensuring that we respect our audience's autonomy and uphold the integrity of our profession.

1. Understanding the Difference: Persuasion vs. Manipulation

   At first glance, persuasion and manipulation might seem synonymous. Both involve influencing others' attitudes or behaviors. However, they differ in their intent and respect for the individual's autonomy. Persuasion aims to convince others by presenting logical and compelling arguments, allowing them to make informed decisions. Manipulation, however, seeks to control or influence others, often through deceit or coercion, disregarding their autonomy.

2. Upholding Ethical Standards in Social Media Communication

   Lawyers have a responsibility to uphold ethical standards in all our professional activities, including our social media practices. This involves honesty, transparency, and respect for our audience's autonomy. We must ensure that our content is truthful, clear, and does not mislead or exploit our audience.

3. The Power and Responsibility of Influence

With great power comes great responsibility. As we gain followers and influence on social media, we must use this power responsibly. We should strive to educate, inform, and inspire our audience, rather than coerce or deceive them into action.

4. Transparency in Advertising and Sponsorships

Transparency is key when it comes to advertising and sponsorships. If we're promoting a product or service, or if we have a partnership or sponsorship arrangement, it's crucial to disclose this to our audience. Not only is this an ethical obligation, but in many jurisdictions, it's also a legal requirement.

5. Avoiding Misrepresentation and Over-Promising

When discussing legal matters, it's essential to avoid misrepresentation or over-promising. Law is complex, and outcomes can rarely be guaranteed. We should strive to provide accurate and realistic information, helping our audience understand that each case is unique and subject to many variables.

6. Respecting Privacy and Confidentiality

Respect for privacy and confidentiality is a fundamental principle in law, and it extends to our social media activities. We must ensure that any client stories or case details we share do not breach confidentiality or privacy rights. This includes anonymizing details or obtaining explicit consent where necessary.

7. Mindful Engagement and Responsiveness

Engaging with our audience is an integral part of social media, but we must do so mindfully. We should strive to provide helpful and respectful responses, but avoid offering specific legal advice that could inadvertently create a lawyer-client relationship.

8. Continuous Learning and Adaptation

Ethics in social media is a rapidly evolving field, with new technologies, platforms, and issues emerging regularly. As responsible professionals, we must commit to continuous learning and adaptation, staying informed about the latest developments and best practices in digital ethics.

In conclusion, navigating the fine line between persuasion and manipulation in social media is a delicate but crucial task. By upholding ethical standards, respecting our audience's autonomy, and committing to transparency, honesty, and continuous learning, we can use social media to positively influence, educate, and advocate, while maintaining the trust and respect of our audience.

Chapter 20

Staying Ahead of the Curve: Future Trends in Short Form Video

The world of short form video is fast-paced and ever-evolving. As a personal injury lawyer, you must stay ahead of the curve, understanding and anticipating future trends to maximize our impact on these platforms. The following are key trends to watch out for and incorporate into your short form video strategy.

1. Augmented Reality (AR) and Virtual Reality (VR):

    AR and VR technologies are set to revolutionize the way we create and consume content. With platforms like Instagram already offering AR filters, and VR technology becoming increasingly accessible, these tools offer innovative ways to engage audiences in immersive experiences. Imagine a VR video that lets users experience a day in your law firm, or an AR filter that helps explain complex legal concepts.

2. AI-Generated Content:

    Artificial intelligence is making significant strides in content creation. AI tools can now generate scripts, edit videos, and even predict what kind of content will perform well. Embracing these tools can help streamline your content creation process and optimize your videos for success.

Email me directly at mike@mikekruzich.com if you would like me to personally assess your Lawfirm's social media presence.

3. Personalized Content:

   As algorithms become more sophisticated, they're increasingly able to serve users with content tailored to their interests and preferences. This means that creating personalized content, which speaks directly to your target audience's needs and concerns, will be more important than ever.

4. Interactive Content:

   Interactive content is set to become a significant trend in short form video. This includes videos that incorporate polls, quizzes, or choose-your-own-adventure style narratives. Interactive content can boost engagement and give you valuable insights into your audience's preferences.

5. Sustainability and Social Responsibility:

   As consumers become more conscious of social and environmental issues, they're increasingly seeking out brands that align with their values. Videos that showcase your law firm's commitment to sustainability or social responsibility can help build trust and connection with your audience.

6. Voice and Visual Search:

   With the rise of voice assistants and visual search technology, optimizing your videos for voice and visual search will be crucial. This means using clear, descriptive titles and tags, and considering how users might describe your video when speaking or using visual search.

7. Live Streaming and Real-Time Engagement:

    Live streaming is already a significant trend in short form video, and it's set to grow even more. Live streams offer a unique opportunity for real-time engagement, allowing you to answer questions, respond to comments, and build a deeper connection with your audience.

8. User-Generated Content (UGC):

    UGC, such as testimonials or stories from your clients, can be a powerful tool for building trust and authenticity. Encouraging and incorporating UGC into your video strategy can help foster a sense of community around your brand.

9. Short Form Video Advertising:

    As short form video continues to grow, so too will opportunities for video advertising. Understanding the unique characteristics and requirements of short form video ads will be crucial for maximizing your reach and impact.

10. Cross-Platform Integration:

    Lastly, cross-platform integration will become increasingly important. This means not only sharing your videos across different platforms but also understanding each platform's unique features and adapting your content accordingly.

In conclusion, staying ahead of the curve in the world of short form video requires a commitment to continuous learning and adaptation. By keeping an eye on these future trends, you can ensure that your video strategy remains cutting-edge, engaging, and effective in reaching your audience.

Chapter 21

The Million-Follower Blueprint: Your Roadmap to Social Media Dominance

Building a substantial following on social media isn't easy. It requires strategy, consistency, and an understanding of your audience's wants and needs. In this chapter, I'll share my journey of amassing a million followers in under six months, providing you with a practical roadmap to social media dominance.

1. Starting from Scratch: The Importance of a Solid Foundation

   When I started, I didn't have a following. Like many of you, I was at zero, trying to figure out the best approach. The key is to lay a solid foundation: defining your niche, understanding your target audience, and establishing a consistent brand identity. These elements serve as the guiding principles for your content creation and interaction with your audience.

2. The Power of Consistency: Why Posting Frequency Matters

   One of the significant factors in my rapid growth was posting frequency. I was posting several times per day. This consistency served two primary purposes: it gave my audience regular touchpoints with my brand, and it sent signals to the platform algorithms that I was an active and reliable content creator, which in turn increased the visibility of my content.

3. Understanding Your Audience: The Key to Engaging Content

I quickly learned that to engage my audience effectively, I needed to understand them deeply. What were their interests? What problems were they facing? What kind of content did they find valuable and enjoyable? By answering these questions, I could create content that resonated with my audience and encouraged interaction.

4. Data-Driven Decisions: The Role of Analytics in Content Strategy

Crucially, my strategy wasn't based on guesswork or intuition. It was driven by data. I closely monitored my analytics, tracking which types of content performed best, when my audience was most active, and what topics generated the most engagement. This data allowed me to refine my content strategy continually, focusing on what worked and discarding what didn't.

5. Staying True to Your Niche: Building Authority and Trust

While it was tempting to jump on every trend or diversify my content, I found that staying true to my niche was more beneficial. By consistently posting relevant content, I was able to build my authority in my field and gain my audience's trust. Remember, people follow you because they're interested in your specific niche, not because they want to see popular content that they can find anywhere else.

6. Engaging with Your Audience: Building a Community

Growing a following isn't just about broadcasting content; it's about building a community. I made a point to engage with my audience regularly, responding to comments, asking for feedback, and showing appreciation for their support. This engagement helped build a sense of community and fostered a deeper connection with my audience.

7. Adapting and Evolving: Staying Ahead of the Curve

Finally, while consistency and data-driven decision-making were crucial, so too was the ability to adapt and evolve. Social media trends change rapidly, and staying ahead of the curve is essential for maintaining growth and engagement. I regularly reassessed my strategy, stayed informed about new features and trends, and wasn't afraid to experiment with new content formats.

In conclusion, achieving social media dominance isn't about overnight success or viral hits. It's about laying a solid foundation, understanding your audience, making data-driven decisions, posting consistently, and being willing to adapt and evolve. This roadmap isn't a quick fix, but it's a proven strategy for building a substantial

Email me directly at mike@mikekruzich.com if you
would like me to personally assess your Lawfirm's social media presence

and engaged following. Remember, the journey to a million followers begins with a single post. Start creating, start posting, and start building your own path to social media dominance today.

Chapter 22

Going Beyond Short Form Video: How to Repurpose Your Short Form Into Any Type of Content On Any Platform

Creating content that resonates with your audience is an art, but it doesn't have to be a one-time masterpiece. In fact, some of your best work can be repurposed and reshaped to fit various platforms and formats. After mastering short-form videos, the next step is leveraging this content to expand your digital presence across multiple platforms. Let's explore how to accomplish this.

1. Long Form YouTube Videos

    Short form videos can serve as the building blocks for longer YouTube videos. A compilation of 3-5 short-form videos can easily turn into a 3-minute long-form video, or you can delve deeper into a topic that performed well in a short-form video. The advantage of YouTube is its longevity – a well-optimized video can continue to get views and engagement long after it was first published. However, it's worth noting that the platform requires more time and resources than short-form video platforms. Also, unlike short-form platforms, where content is pushed to viewers through algorithms, YouTube requires a more proactive approach to promotion and SEO.

2. Twitter Posts

    Twitter is the home of bite-sized content, making it the perfect platform for repurposing short-form videos. Your best punchlines, insights, or advice can be extracted from your videos and turned into Twitter posts. The beauty of Twitter lies in its real-time, conversational nature, allowing you to engage directly with your audience. However, its fast-paced nature can also be a disadvantage, as content can quickly get lost in the sea of tweets, necessitating regular posting to maintain visibility.

3. LinkedIn Posts

    LinkedIn is another excellent platform for repurposing short-form video content. Transforming your video content into informational posts or articles can help establish your authority and expertise in the legal field. LinkedIn's professional audience is likely to appreciate and engage with in-depth, valuable content. However, LinkedIn requires a more formal tone and professional approach, which may not be suitable for all types of content.

4. Blog Posts

    Turning your short-form video content into blog posts for your website can significantly boost your SEO, particularly for long-tail keywords. By converting your video content into written form, you can target specific keywords and phrases that potential clients might be using to find legal services. The search intent on Google is high, meaning that people who find your content are actively seeking information or solutions, making them high-quality leads. The downside is that SEO takes time and consistent effort, and it may take several months to see significant results.

5. The Marketing Flywheel

Leveraging all these platforms can create a powerful marketing flywheel. A flywheel is a self-reinforcing cycle where each part feeds and accelerates the next. In this context, short-form videos are your engine. They are quick to create, easy to digest, and have a high potential for virality. These videos can be repurposed into different formats for different platforms, each reinforcing your brand and drawing more attention back to your original content. This cycle of creation, repurposing, and cross-promotion can drive significant growth over time.

For personal injury lawyers, this flywheel can be a game-changer. It allows you to reach a wider audience, establish your expertise, and attract high-quality leads. It also maximizes your content creation efforts by repurposing a single piece of content into various formats, saving time and resources.

In conclusion, mastering short-form video is just the beginning. By repurposing your content for different platforms and formats, you can amplify your reach, engage with your audience in new ways, and ultimately, drive more leads and clients to your practice.

Email me directly at mike@mikekruzich.com if you
would like me to personally assess your Lawfirm's social media presence

It's about working smarter, not harder. It's about leveraging every piece of content to its fullest potential and tapping into the power of the marketing flywheel. With this approach, you can truly dominate the digital landscape and establish yourself as a leading personal injury lawyer in the world of social media.

Bonus Chapter 1

101 Content Ideas for Personal Injury Lawyers

Content creation can be a daunting task, especially when you're trying to maintain a steady stream of fresh, engaging videos for your audience. To help you overcome this challenge, here are 101 content ideas tailored specifically for personal injury lawyers.

The key to successful content creation is consistency, authenticity, and providing value to your audience. Always keep your audience's needs and interests at the forefront of your content strategy, and you'll be on your way to building a powerful social media presence.

Remember, these are ideas to spark your creativity. Make each one your own, infusing your unique perspective and voice. It's about creating a connection with your audience and offering them real value in a format that's accessible and engaging. That's the true power of short-form video for personal injury lawyers.

1. Client testimonials: Share stories of satisfied clients (with their consent, of course). This can help build trust and show potential clients what they can expect when they choose your firm.

2. Common misconceptions about personal injury law: Address common misconceptions or myths to educate your audience.

3. Case studies: Discuss past cases (anonymized) to demonstrate your expertise.

4. Interviews with team members: Introduce your team members and their roles.

5. FAQs: Answer commonly asked questions about personal injury law.

6. Day in the life: Show what a typical day looks like in your law firm.

7. Safety tips: Share tips on how to prevent common accidents.

8. Legal jargon explained: Break down complex legal terms into layman's language.

9. Statistics: Share interesting statistics related to personal injury law.

10. Updates on laws: Discuss changes in laws that might affect your audience.

11. Tips on what to do after an accident: Important steps people often miss or do not know about.

12. Behind the scenes in court: Share insights on what happens in court during a personal injury case.

13. Understanding compensation: Explain the factors that contribute to the amount of compensation one can receive.

14. Debunking stereotypes about personal injury claims: Address the negative perception some people have towards personal injury claims.

15. Effects of personal injuries: Discuss the physical, mental, and financial impacts.

16. Public place injuries: Discuss potential hazards in public spaces and how people can protect their rights.

17. Workplace safety: Share information about workplace injuries and workers' compensation rights.

18. Medical malpractice: Provide insight into medical malpractice cases and how to recognize them.

19. Personal injury law in news: Discuss a recent news story related to personal injury law.

20. The role of insurance companies: Explain how insurance companies factor into personal injury claims.

21. Collaborations with other professionals: Partner with medical professionals or therapists to discuss recovery from personal injuries.

22. Injury prevention gadgets: Showcase and review gadgets or equipment that can help prevent injuries.

23. Celebrating wins: Without sharing sensitive information, celebrate the success of a case or a milestone for your firm.

24. Discussing landmark personal injury cases: Discuss previous significant cases in your jurisdiction or internationally.

25. Sharing motivational quotes: Share inspiring quotes that can help motivate and uplift those going through a challenging time after an injury.

26. Community involvement: Highlight your law firm's involvement in local community events or charities.

27. Client journey: With the client's permission, document their journey through a case, from the initial consultation to the resolution.

28. The importance of evidence in personal injury cases: Discuss how evidence is used and why it's crucial to keep records and documents.

29. How personal injury law differs from other law fields: Highlight the unique aspects of personal injury law, compared to criminal law, corporate law, etc.

30. The history of personal injury law: Share some interesting historical facts about the development of personal injury law.

31. The future of personal injury law: Discuss emerging trends and what the future might look like in this field.

32. Responding to audience questions: Make a video responding directly to questions or comments from your followers. This not only engages your audience but also gives you a constant source of content ideas based on what your audience wants to know.

33. Understanding 'No Win, No Fee': Explain how contingency fees work.

34. How to choose a personal injury lawyer: Provide guidance on what factors to consider.

35. How to file a personal injury claim: Step-by-step guide.

36. Exploring different types of personal injuries: Each video could focus on a different type of injury.

37. Highlighting local resources for accident victims: For instance, support groups, rehabilitation centers, etc.

38. Explaining the role of negligence in personal injury cases: Distinguish between negligence and intentional harm.

39. Importance of medical documentation: Explain why keeping detailed medical records is crucial.

40. Recognizing signs of a concussion: Discuss the signs and symptoms of a common injury like a concussion.

41. What to know about wrongful death lawsuits: Discuss the sensitive topic of wrongful death cases.

42. How long does a personal injury case take: Explain the timeline of a typical case.

43. How to document a car accident scene: Share tips on gathering evidence at the scene.

44. Choosing the right medical treatment after an accident: Provide guidance on seeking treatment.

45. Pre-existing conditions and your personal injury claim: Discuss how pre-existing conditions can impact a claim.

46. The statute of limitations for personal injury cases: Break down the time frame for filing a lawsuit.

47. The connection between personal injury and mental health: Discuss topics like emotional distress in personal injury cases.

48. Dealing with insurance adjusters: Share tips on how to handle discussions with insurance adjusters.

49. Understanding settlements: Explain what a settlement is and how it works.

50. The pros and cons of going to trial: Discuss why some cases go to trial and others do not.

51. What is a deposition: Explain the process of a deposition in a personal injury case.

52. How is pain and suffering calculated: Discuss how courts evaluate "pain and suffering" in monetary terms.

53. Discussing the impact of personal injury on quality of life: Discuss how injuries can impact a person's lifestyle and future.

54. What is comparative negligence? Explaining this concept and how it impacts personal injury cases.

55. The role of expert witnesses in personal injury cases: Discuss how and why expert witnesses are used.

56. Jury vs. judge: Understanding who decides personal injury cases: Explain the differences between a jury trial and a bench trial.

57. The impact of social media on personal injury cases: Discuss how social media can both help and hurt a personal injury case.

58. Slip and fall cases: What you need to know: Discuss common causes and potential injuries from slip and fall accidents.

59. How to handle an injury caused by a defective product: Discuss product liability and related cases.

60. Top 5 misconceptions about personal injury cases: Address common misconceptions about personal injury cases.

61. The truth about pain and suffering damages: Explain what they are and how they're calculated.

62. Busting myths about car accident cases: Address common myths and provide the facts.

63. Understanding punitive damages: Explain what punitive damages are and when they might be awarded.

64. ...

65. The role of a personal injury lawyer during settlement negotiations.

66. Exploring the importance of evidence in personal injury cases: Discuss the types of evidence that can make or break a case.

67. How to handle hit-and-run accidents: Offer advice on what to do if you're a victim of a hit-and-run.

68. What to do if you're injured in a car accident while working: Discuss the intersection of personal injury law and workers' compensation.

69. How to handle an injury from a rental property: Discuss landlord liability and tenant rights.

70. Understanding the impact of personal injury on family members: Discuss how injuries can affect more than just the victim.

71. The role of insurance companies in personal injury cases: Discuss the ways insurance companies get involved in these cases.

72. Explaining the personal injury claim process: A step-by-step walkthrough of what a personal injury claim entails.

73. Unpacking medical malpractice: Discuss what happens when healthcare professionals cause harm.

74. Personal injury claims and bankruptcy: Explain how a personal injury claim can be affected if the victim or defendant files for bankruptcy.

75. Understanding workers' compensation: Discuss the basics of workers' compensation and when employees might need to seek additional legal recourse.

76. The role of police reports in personal injury cases: Discuss how a police report can affect the outcome of a case.

77. What happens when a personal injury occurs on public property: Explain the challenges and considerations in cases involving government entities.

78. When to hire a personal injury lawyer: Offer advice on the best time to seek legal representation.

79. Explaining class action lawsuits: Discuss the circumstances where a class action lawsuit might be appropriate.

80. The impact of COVID-19 on personal injury cases: Discuss how the pandemic has affected case proceedings, including court delays and telehealth evaluations.

81. Understanding dog bite laws: Discuss the responsibility of pet owners in dog bite cases.

82. How to navigate an injury claim without insurance: Offer advice for those who are uninsured or underinsured.

83. The psychological impact of personal injuries: Discuss mental and emotional injuries like PTSD and depression.

84. Explaining the discovery process in personal injury cases: Walk through the steps of the discovery process and why it's crucial.

85. The role of mediation in personal injury cases: Discuss how mediation can be used to resolve disputes and potentially avoid trial.

86. How pre-existing conditions can affect your claim: Discuss the impact of prior health conditions on a personal injury case.

87. The statute of limitations in personal injury cases: Explain the time frame within which a victim must file a claim.

88. How to handle an accident involving a commercial vehicle: Discuss the complexities of accidents involving trucks, taxis, or company cars.

89. The impact of personal injury on quality of life: Discuss the long-term effects of serious injuries.

90. Understanding wrongful death claims: Explain the legal recourse available when a loved one's death is caused by another party's negligence.

91. What to do if you're injured in a pedestrian accident: Offer advice for victims of accidents involving pedestrians and vehicles.

92. How to document your injuries and medical treatment: Provide a guide to effectively documenting injuries and treatments for a personal injury claim.

93. The role of a guardian ad litem in personal injury cases: Discuss how a guardian ad litem can protect the interests of minors or incapacitated adults.

94. How to handle injuries caused by dangerous or defective drugs: Discuss how to navigate cases involving pharmaceutical companies.

95. Understanding vicarious liability: Explain scenarios where one person may be held legally responsible for another's actions, such as an employer for an employee.

96. The role of expert witnesses in personal injury cases: Discuss the importance of experts in building a strong case.

97. Understanding product liability: Discuss cases involving injuries caused by defective or dangerous products.

98. How to handle injuries caused by hazardous materials: Provide advice for cases involving harmful substances at home or work.

99. The impact of personal injury on mental health: Discuss the psychological effects of personal injury, including stress, anxiety, and PTSD.

100. What to do if you're injured at a public event: Offer advice for victims of accidents at concerts, sports games, or other public gatherings.

Email me directly at mike@mikekruzich.com if you
would like me to personally assess your Lawfirm's social media presence

Bonus Chapter 2

"Decoding Twitter: Insights from its Open Source Algorithm"

In an unprecedented move, on March 31, 2023, Twitter opened the doors to its closely guarded algorithm, providing an opportunity for social media strategists, data scientists, and curious individuals to dissect and interpret its content ranking and dissemination mechanisms.

Whether you focus on Twitter or not, the fact remains that since this is the first major platform to ever make their Algorithm open source, we can take the key findings and assume with great confidence that most platforms have similar algorithms. Understanding the social algorithms on this level allows you to tackle content in a scientific way.

For personal injury lawyers, this release presented an opportunity to gain valuable insights on how to optimize their content for maximum reach and engagement on the platform. This chapter seeks to outline some of the main findings from the open-source Twitter algorithm and how these can be utilized to enhance your Twitter strategy.

Understanding the Twitter Algorithm

1. Recency Matters: It's no secret that Twitter is a fast-paced platform, but the open source algorithm confirmed that recency is a significant factor. This highlights the importance of timely posts, reacting to news and trends in real time.

2. Engagement Is Key: Unsurprisingly, engagement in the form of likes, retweets, and replies significantly influence a tweet's visibility. Crafting tweets that encourage interaction from your audience will increase the likelihood of your tweets being seen by more people.

3. Relevance to User Interests: The algorithm takes into account a user's past behavior, including the type of content they interact with and the accounts they follow. This means you must maintain a clear, consistent theme in your tweets to increase the chances of being seen by your target audience.

4. Diversity of Content Sources: The algorithm attempts to show users a variety of content from different sources, giving an advantage to content that stands out from the norm.

The Heavy-Ranker Algorithm Weight Per Action

Programmer Steven Tey said it like this:

"There are a few factors that determine if your tweet will appear on someone's "For You" page.

These are calculated by a heavy-ranker algorithm, which receives various features describing the Tweet + the user whose timeline is being ranked for, and outputs binary predictions about how the user will engage with the Tweet.

Below are some of the probabilities that the algorithm outputs, along with their respective sentiments and weights:"

User Action	Sentiment	Weight
Like your tweet	Positive	0.5
Retweet your tweet	Positive	1
Click into your tweet & reply/like a tweet or stay there for >2 mins	Positive	11
Check out your profile and like/reply to a tweet	Positive	12
Reply to your tweet	Positive	27
Reply to your tweet and you engage with this reply	Positive	75
Request "show less often" on your Tweet/you, block or mute you	Negative	-74
Report your Tweet	Negative	-369

Applying the Findings

As a personal injury lawyer, understanding these findings can help you elevate your Twitter strategy.

Post timely content: Stay up-to-date with current events and trends related to personal injury law. Use trending hashtags where appropriate to increase the visibility of your tweets.

Engage your audience: Encourage interaction from your audience by asking questions, seeking opinions, or creating polls. Remember to engage back, reply to comments and interact with your followers.

Email me directly at mike@mikekruzich.com if you
would like me to personally assess your Lawfirm's social media presence

Maintain a clear theme: Stick to topics that are relevant to your field and your target audience. This will increase the likelihood of your tweets being seen by potential clients and other individuals interested in personal injury law.

Diversify your content: Don't limit yourself to text-only tweets. Share relevant articles, infographics, videos, and even quotes to keep your content fresh and engaging.

Twitter's decision to make its algorithm open source has given us an invaluable tool for understanding how to make the most of the platform. The insights gleaned from the algorithm can help you refine your strategy and gain an edge in the highly competitive Twitterverse. Keep in mind, however, that while understanding the algorithm is important, ultimately the key to Twitter success is creating high-quality, relevant, and engaging content for your followers.